THE FABER BOOK OF MONOLOGUES FOR MEN

Jane Edwardes is the Theatre Editor for *Time Out* magazine.

THE FABER BOOK OF
Monologues for Men

INTRODUCED WITH NOTES AND COMMENTARIES
BY JANE EDWARDES

faber and faber

First published in 2005
by Faber and Faber Limited
3 Queen Square London WC1N 3AU
Published in the United States by Faber and Faber Inc.
an affiliate of Farrar, Straus and Giroux LLC, New York

Typeset by Country Setting, Kingsdown, Kent CT14 8ES
Printed in England by Mackays of Chatham plc, Chatham, Kent

A CIP record for this book is available from the British Library

ISBN 0-571-21764-8

2 4 6 8 10 9 7 5 3 1

Contents

I would like to thank all the actors and directors who talked to me about their experiences of auditioning, especially Declan Donnellan, Nicolas Kent, Max Stafford-Clark and Deborah Warner; Pamela Edwardes, Nicolas Kent again, and Andrew Powell for reading the manuscript; Peggy Paterson at Faber for all her support and encouragement; and, lastly, the dramatists whose plays I have had the pleasure of seeing and reading over many years. All mistakes are, of course, my own.

Introduction

These twenty-five modern monologues are designed for male performers of all ages and a variety of accents. They have been chosen because they have an emotional drive and energy, are revealing of character, and, in many cases, tell a compelling story. Long, informative pieces have been avoided. Nobody in their right mind would choose the Archbishop of Canterbury's speech disentangling the legal justification for going to war in Shakespeare's *Henry V*; even the most extraordinary of actors struggle to make it interesting. The earliest play is Errol John's *Moon on a Rainbow Shawl*, seen in its first version in 1958 and frequently revived. Some extracts are drawn from established playwrights, others from the less well known and up-and-coming. All the plays have been produced in Britain – several of them all over the world – mostly beginning their careers at theatres like the Royal Court and the Bush in London or the Traverse in Edinburgh, theatres that concentrate on new writing.

Out of interest, the names of the performers who first spoke the words onstage have been included in the introductions, although that doesn't mean that you have to look like them, or that there are not different ways of playing the part. The short introductions also provide a bit of background to the play, the crucial aspects of the plot, and something about the point at which the extract occurs, and to whom the character is talking. Where there are interjections, these have been removed to help the flow of the speech. Of course, it can't be stressed strongly enough that once you have looked through this book and, I hope, found a speech that appeals to you, it is essential to get hold of the play text in order to understand the character as fully as you possibly can. In some cases, it is best to look for a character who is no more than five years older or younger than you are yourself. Equally, don't choose a speech written in a different accent from your own unless you are very confident that you can pull it off.

Auditioning is a demanding process for everyone, and that includes those who are sitting in judgement: the directors, casting directors, producers, or examiners. If the audition is for a particular production, they know that a single mistake can doom their production to failure. Even the most brilliant director can't rescue a production that has been badly mis-cast. They are not only interested in choosing those who will be able to play the parts, but also those who will make a posi-tive contribution to the rehearsal process. For the actors there is the fear of rejection. It's hardly surprising if, under the nervousness, many are furious that they have to put themselves repeatedly through this ordeal. But Declan Donnellan, the artistic director of Cheek by Jowl, pointed out to me during research for this book that if auditions didn't exist, directors would repeatedly work with familiar faces, and the opportunities for new people would diminish.

An audition may be for a specific part, or with a view to joining a company putting on a number of plays, or it may be part of an exam, an entry requirement to a course, or a com-petition. In the first case you may also be required to read from the script. Some directors say that they have made up their minds within seconds of seeing the actor because they have a very clear idea of what they are looking for. Short of having plastic surgery, changing your genetic structure, or reliving your life, there's not a lot you can do about that. It may be that there's a part you could just make at a stretch and the director is enthusiastic at the time; but there's always the possibility that someone else will come in later and hit the bull's eye. If you don't get the job there's no point in wasting time on won-dering whether you were rejected because you didn't smile at the right person, or because that witty riposte occurred to you on the tube going home, rather than in the audition room.

There are, however, things you can do to help yourself prepare, apart from putting in as much work as possible on the speech. Give some thought to how you are going to dress, choosing clean and comfortable clothes, nothing too formal or too casual. Treat the audition as beginning from the moment you walk into the room. Most especially, prepare the introduction to the speech as well as the speech itself. Give the name of the play, the playwright and the context in which the character finds himself before the speech begins. If you don't do that, half of your audience's attention may be taken up with trying to work out what is going on rather than assessing your talent. Don't embarrass one person by addressing the entire speech to them. If the speech is to the audience, then embrace them all; if to an imaginary character or characters, take some time to establish where they are to help the audience visualise them. If, after you have finished, the director chooses to work on the piece with you, then show that you are open to suggestion and aware that a piece may be played in many different ways. Above all, remember that auditioning makes everyone nervous, not just you. Don't try and fight it but rather – and this is easier said than done – try to use that nervous energy creatively instead. Good luck!

Monologues for Men

'Art'

YASMINA REZA

First produced in this translation by Christopher Hampton at Wyndham's Theatre, London, in 1996 with Ken Stott as Yvan.

Yasmina Reza's *'Art'* has played all over the world. In London, in particular, its long run has offered the chance for a variety of actors of all ages to play the roles of the three men whose friendship is almost destroyed by the purchase of a white canvas with some fine white diagonal lines for the hefty sum of 200,000 French francs. Why does Marc feel personally insulted by Serge's quixotic purchase? Surely there are far worse things that he could have done? As the two egoists battle it out, one man is caught in the middle, and the actors fortunate enough to have played this part have quickly discovered that they were in prime position to walk away with the play. Not that Yvan would ever do anything so aggressive himself. He is the classic conciliator, who desperately wants to keep the peace, even if it means concealing his true feelings about both the painting and his friends. He lives in constant danger of Serge and Marc uniting against him, but they are more accustomed to pitying Yvan, particularly as the chaos of his home life reaches a climax during the preparations for his marriage. He is late for an evening with the pair when he storms in and gives this speech, barely pausing for breath as he recounts the impossibility of keeping all branches of his own and his future bride's family happy. It's a long speech – now a very famous one – but delivered at a hectic pace, and it invariably sweeps the audience along with its sudden injection of energy. In London, *'Art'* became known as the perfect West End play: provocative, funny and short. Yasmina Reza won the *Evening Standard*

Award for Best Comedy: at the ceremony, she pronounced herself grateful but bemused since she was under the impression that she had written a tragedy.

'ART'

Yvan So, a crisis, insoluble problem, major crisis, both stepmothers want their names on the wedding invitation. Catherine adores her stepmother, who more or less brought her up, she wants her name on the invitation, she wants it and her stepmother is not anticipating, which is understandable, since the mother is dead, not appearing next to Catherine's father, whereas my stepmother, whom I detest, it's out of the question her name should appear on the invitation, but my father won't have his name on it if hers isn't, unless Catherine's stepmother's is left off, which is completely unacceptable, I suggested none of the parents' names should be on it, after all we're not adolescents, we can announce our wedding and invite people ourselves, so Catherine screamed her head off, arguing that would be a slap in the face for her parents, who were paying through the nose for the reception, and particularly for her stepmother, who's gone to so much trouble when she isn't even her daughter, and I finally let myself be persuaded, totally against my better judgement, because she wore me down, I finally agreed that my stepmother, whom I detest, who's a complete bitch, will have her name on the invitation, so I telephoned my mother to warn her, Mother, I said, I've done everything I can to avoid this, but we have absolutely no choice, Yvonne's name has to be on the invitation, she said, if Yvonne's name is on the invitation, take mine off it, Mother, I said, please, I beg you, don't make things even more difficult, and she said, how dare you suggest my name is left to float around the card on its own, as if I was some abandoned woman, below Yvonne, who'll be clamped onto your father's surname, like a limpet, I said to her, Mother, I have friends waiting for me, I'm going to hang up and

we'll discuss all this tomorrow after a good night's sleep,
she said, why is it I'm always an afterthought, what are you
talking about, Mother, you're not always an afterthought,
of course I am and when you say don't make things even
more difficult, what you mean is, everything's already been
decided, everything's been organised without me, everything's
been cooked up behind my back, good old Huguette, she'll
agree to anything and all this, she said – to put the old tin
lid on it – in aid of an event, the importance of which I'm
having some trouble grasping, Mother, I have friends
waiting for me, that's right, there's always something better
to do, anything's more important than I am, goodbye, and
she hung up, Catherine, who was next to me, but who
hadn't heard her side of the conversation, said, what did
she say, I said, she doesn't want her name on the invitation
with Yvonne, which is understandable, I'm not talking
about that, what was it she said about the wedding,
nothing, you're lying, I'm not, Cathy, I promise you, she
just doesn't want her name on the invitation with Yvonne,
call her back and tell her when your son's getting married,
you rise above your vanity, you could say the same thing to
your stepmother, that's got nothing to do with it, Catherine
shouted, it's me, I'm the one who's insisting her name's on
it, it's not her, poor thing, she's tact personified, if she had
any idea of the problem this is causing, she'd be down
on her knees, begging for her name to be taken off the
invitation, now call your mother, so I called her again, by
now I'm in shreds, Catherine's listening on the extension,
Yvan, my mother says, up to now you've conducted your
affairs in the most chaotic way imaginable and just because,
out of the blue, you've decided to embark on matrimony,
I find myself obliged to spend all afternoon and evening
with your father, a man I haven't seen for seventeen years
and to whom I was not expecting to have to reveal my hip-
size and my puffy cheeks, not to mention Yvonne who
incidentally, I may tell you, according to Félix Perolari, has

now taken up bridge – my mother also plays bridge – I can see none of this can be helped, but on the invitation, the one item everyone is going to receive and examine, I insist on making a solo appearance, Catherine, listening on the extension, shakes her head and screws up her face in disgust, Mother, I say, why are you so selfish, I'm not selfish, I'm not selfish, Yvan, you're not going to start as well, you're not going to be like Mme Roméro this morning and tell me I have a heart of stone, that everybody in our family has a heart of stone, that's what Mme Roméro said this morning when I refused to raise her wages – she's gone completely mad, by the way – to sixty francs an hour tax-free, she had the gall to say everyone in the family had a heart of stone, when she knows very well about poor André's pacemaker, you haven't even bothered to drop him a line, yes, that's right, very funny, everything's a joke to you, it's not me who's the selfish one, Yvan, you've still got a lot to learn about life, off you go, my boy, go on, go on, go and see your precious friends . . .

Silence.

Then nothing. Nothing's been resolved. I hung up. Mini-drama with Catherine. Cut short, because I was late.

Bash

NEIL LABUTE

*First produced at the Douglas Fairbanks Theatre, New
York, with Matthew Lillard as John, then transferred to
the Almeida Theatre, London.*

Don't attempt this unless you are entirely confident of your
Boston accent! 'A Gaggle of Saints' is one of three short plays
by the American Neil LaBute that make up *Bash*. LaBute's
black and controversial films – *In the Company of Men* and
Your Friends and Neighbours – had already made a stir when
these plays were first staged. Like the characters in his play,
LaBute was once a Mormon student himself, albeit a thorn
in his church's side. Interrupting, half-acknowledging each
other, John and Sue (such bland names!) give their own versions – one repellent, the other romantic – of an eventful
evening in Manhattan. Their evening dress contrasts strangely
with John's brutal story. They have been engaged for six
years without sleeping together. John is super-fit and prone
to violence. They come to New York with friends for a student
ball at the Plaza. Beforehand they go for a stroll in Central
Park on a perfect October night. While enjoying the peace
and calm of the park, John notices with disgust a couple of
gays coming out of the bushes. Later, in the early hours of
the morning after a wonderful evening and as the women are
sleeping, he suggests to his male companions that they should
return to the Park. Once again, they spot a couple of men
canoodling. Enraged as much by the men's brazen lack of
guilt as anything else, John follows one of them into the men's
room and the horrific events he describes below take place.

John is not someone to question his church's condem-
nation of homosexuality. He is besotted with the beauty of
his girlfriend in her party frock, but his reaction to the gay

men is so violent that it's impossible not to wonder whether he fears he is gay himself. The unnerving thing for the members of the audience is that John assumes they will share his disgust.

John before going in i told the guys to hold off, wait out
here for me till they got my signal . . . and that's the plan.
wait for me to flush him out, make sure no one wanders
by. when i get inside, 's like another world . . . walls are
exploding with graffiti. place stinks. two bulbs burnt out.
some old dude curled up, asleep in a corner. and our
friend's legs, i spot, patiently sitting in a stall. waiting, and
not a care in this world. i slip into the booth next to his,
start fumbling with my belt, this, that, and like clockwork,
this guy's hand comes up under my side of the partition. his
signal. pink fingers, wiggling up at me. imploring. i notice
this thin gold band on his little finger, catching the light.
(*Beat.*) so, i lay my open palm in his and two minutes later
we're standing near the mirrors – big pieces of stainless
steel, really – standing, and sizing each other up. small talk.
'name's chet,' he says, and i don't even bat an eyelash as he
moves in, his lips playing across my cheek. let his tongue
run along my teeth and a hand, free hand, tracing down my
fly . . . i just smile at him, smile and even lick his chin for a
second, for a single second. i see his shoulders relax. then
i whistle. i let out a whistle that sends him stumbling back,
blinking, and kind of waving his hands in the air as tim and
dave appear in the doorway. he looks at them, looks and
comes back from his fantasies long enough to touch down
on earth, a flicker in his eyes, realising no good can come
from this . . . and starts babbling. this guy, 'chet', probably
a vp some bank on park avenue, and he's babbling and
wetting himself like an infant. i don't remember exactly, but
i think he even got on his knees, down on his knees and the
pleading. begging. (*Beat.*) my first shot catches him against
the cheek, just under the eye and he slams into a sink. all

snot and blood running down. with so many of us hitting, tearing at him, it's hard to get off a clean punch but i know i connect a few more times. i feel his head, the back of it, softening as we go, but i just find a new spot and move on. tim kicking him long after he's blacked out . . .

Pause.

finally, we start to relax a bit, looking at what we've done. exhausted. spent. i mean, this man is not moving, may never move again and we know it's time to leave. believe this, guy in the corner, sleeps through it all?! (*Beat.*) before we go, tim leans into it one more time, takes a little run at it, smashing his foot against the bridge of this man's nose and i see it give way. just pick up and move to the other side of his face. wow. and then it's silence. not a sound. and for the first time, we look over at dave. tim and me. i mean, really look at him. us together, tim, myself, that's one thing, it's unspoken, our bond, but we don't know david. don't really know him . . . what's he thinking? and right then, as if to answer us through revelation . . . he grabs up the nearest trash can, big wire mesh thing, raises it above his head as he whispers, 'fag.' i'll never forget that . . . 'fag.' that's all. and brings that can down right on the spine of the guy, who just sort of shudders a bit, expelling some air. boom! right on his back, as i'm leaning down, pulling that ring off his pinkie. (*Beat.*) i told you i noticed it . . .

Pause.

then, and i still can't even believe this, then tim does the most amazing thing. this'll go down, the record books. there, with the three of us over this guy's body, he pulls out his key chain, opens the little cylinder he's got dangling on the end of it, and dumps the last of his oil, consecrated oil, on this dude's forehead! i'm not kidding . . . dumps it and starts offering up a short blessing. i mean, i'm getting delirious, this is, like, almost surreal . . . and halfway

through, tim's praying along, we all start giggling. like
schoolboys, we're howling, tears running down, can't catch
our breath we find it all so funny! and that's how we leave
him . . . (*Beat.*) slip out, one by one, running back toward
the plaza in the dark and whooping it up like indians. war
cries, and running with just a trace of moonlight dancing
off the pond as we go . . .

Butley

SIMON GRAY

*First produced at the Criterion Theatre, London, in 1971
with Alan Bates as Butley.*

Although Simon Gray is an enormously prolific playwright,
Butley, first seen in a production directed by his friend Harold
Pinter, is still his best-known play, largely because it was made
into a film with Alan Bates reprising his stage performance in
the title role. Bates, who won awards in both London and
New York for his performance, said at the time that the part
demanded huge amounts of energy, even more than Hamlet,
a role he played in the same year.

Ben Butley is a lecturer in English Literature at London
University, as was Gray when he wrote this play. The action
is confined to a single place – a study shared by Butley and
Joey – and a single day. During the course of this day, Butley
hears three things that upset him: that his estranged wife
is marrying someone he believes to be 'the most boring man
in London'; that Joey, a male protégé, is moving in with his
boyfriend; and that he is in trouble with his head of department. Butley brings all this on his own head for, like so many
of Gray's characters, he is enormously self-destructive, hugely
selfish, and given to lashing out at others. His savage wit and
unrepressed honesty are painful for those on the receiving end
but often outrageously funny for the audience. He drinks too
much, smokes even more, and is cavalier with his students.
In the past he was clearly an inspirational teacher, but now
he takes no pains to hide his contempt for the mediocre
students who knock on his door. He adores Joey, once a
favoured student, who has since become a lecturer himself
and now shares his office. Although there is nothing in the
play to say that Butley and Joey were ever lovers, Butley is

nevertheless enormously upset by Joey's relationship with Reg. Since Butley's wife left, he and Joey have been sharing a flat, but the latter is struggling to escape the older man's influence and planning to move in with his boyfriend; something that Butley has yet to find out when he makes the typically aggressive speech that follows, in which he questions Joey about his life with Reg.

Ben He seemed an amiable sort of chap the one time I met him, even though his mouth was full of symbolic sausage and his fist around a tankard of something foaming symbolically. I had the impression that most people would like him. And as he seemed exactly like most people, only from the North, ergo, he'd be favourably disposed towards himself only more so, or not?

He smiles. Joey also smiles.

Tell me, does he ever discuss his work with you? Or does he leave it behind him at the office? When you go around for one of those little dinners, does he put his feet up, perhaps, while you slave away over a hot stove, or does he do the cooking? No, I don't mean to probe – or am I prying? For instance, in our professor's ménage Hazel rips the meat apart with saw-edged knives while James brews up sauces from *Guardian* headlines. In my ménage, when I had one – remember? – Anne under-grilled the chops and over-boiled the peas while I drank the wine and charted my dropping sugar-count. Now that you and I are sharing my life again I open the tins and you stir the Nescafé again, just as we always used to do, those evenings, at least, when you're not cooking for Reg or Reg isn't cooking for you – which, arriving where we began, does it happen to be? And if it's the former, why, now I think of it, have you never cooked for me, do you think?

Comedians

TREVOR GRIFFITHS

First produced at the Nottingham Playhouse, Nottingham, in 1975 with Jonathan Pryce as Gethin Price.

Eddie Waters (played in the first production by the comedian Jimmy Jewel) is a humanist, an old comic who is generously imparting his skills to a group of working-class would-be comedians. He teaches them to look for the truth: the implication is that society can be changed by persuasion. He also teaches them to avoid comedy that reinforces stereotypes, that attacks gays, the Irish, women or Pakistanis. Trevor Griffiths's play pre-dated the rise of alternative comedy in the eighties. Waters' students are due to perform their acts to Challenor, an old foe of Waters who could offer the most talented members of the group a contract to play the working men's clubs. The play takes place in two venues: the classroom where the evening class is held; at the bingo hall where they perform; and then back in the classroom after the performance. Challenor gives them a pep talk beforehand and insists on the need to be entertaining, that the audience is their paymaster, and Max Bygraves the ultimate standard. Torn between Waters' and Challenor's opposing views, most of the class crumble, ditching what they have learnt under Waters in the hope of escaping their dead-end jobs. Gethin Price (Jonathan Pryce in a landmark role in his career) also unexpectedly performs a different act, but this is not to please Challenor, rather because he rejects Waters' liberalism. During the performance, Price, paying tribute to Grock, the famous clown, wears a white face and launches an attack on a pair of dummies, a man and woman in evening dress. He pins a flower on the woman's dress and a patch of blood appears. To Waters' dismay, Price's act is fuelled by hate, lacking in compassion and, as far as Waters is concerned, truth. At the end of a dispiriting evening after the others have left, Waters and Price argue about the purpose of comedy. The raging Price explains that he favours revolution against gradual reform.

Price The truth. Can I say . . . look, I wanna say something. What do you know about the *truth*, Mr Waters? You think the truth is *beautiful*? You've forgotten what it's *like*. You knew it when you started off, Oldham Empire, People's Music Hall, Colne Hippodrome, Bolton Grand, New Brighton Palace, Ardwick Empire, Ardwick Hippodrome, the Met, the Star in Ancoats . . . the Lancashire Lad – you knew it then all right. Nobody hit harder than Eddie Waters, that's what they say. Because you were still in touch with what made you . . . hunger, diphtheria, filth, unemployment, penny clubs, means tests, bed bugs, head lice . . . Was all *that* truth beautiful?

  Pause. Waters stares at him, blinded.

Truth was a fist you hit with. Now it's like . . . now it's like cowflop, a day old, hard until it's underfoot and then it's . . . green, soft. Shitten.

  Pause.

Nothing's changed, Mr Waters, is what I'm saying. When I stand upright – like tonight at that club – I bang my head on the ceiling. Just like you fifty years ago. We're still caged, exploited, prodded and pulled at, milked, fattened, slaughtered, cut up, fed out. We still don't belong to ourselves. Nothing's changed. You've just forgotten, that's all.

  Waters gathers his things about him, using the process.

And you . . . stopped laughing, didn't you? Not even a warm-up tonight. You had nothing to say to those people down there tonight, did you?

Waters turns slowly to face him.

In three months or more, you never said a single funny thing.

Pause.

Challenor reckons you could have been great . . . he said you just stopped wanting it.

Waters sits down heavily at the desk, the pain hurting now.

Maybe you lost your hate, Mr Waters.

A Day in the Death of Joe Egg

PETER NICHOLS

First produced at the Citizens' Theatre, Glasgow, in 1967
with Joe Melia as Bri.

Audiences at the first production of Peter Nichols' *A Day in
the Death of Joe Egg* were taken aback to discover that Peter
Nichols had written a comedy, albeit a black one, about a
couple coping, or rather failing to cope, with their 'human
parsnip', a severely brain-damaged, wheelchair-bound daughter. It's a difficult subject, more likely to be treated with
sticky sentimentality than humour, but this play is rigorously
honest and unsentimental. As far as Bri, a reluctant teacher,
is concerned, it would have been better if Joe had never been
born. Sheila is more caring and optimistic; her problem is
that she has to look after two children – for Bri, outrageously spoilt by his mother, is massively immature and con-
stantly jealous of his wife. Bri and Sheila regularly launch
into an obviously defensive comic double act to the embar-
rassment of any visitors. The audience, too, finds itself cast
in the role of voyeur. Bri adopts another character at the
drop of a hat, whether one of the many doctors they have
been to see in the course of Joe's treatment, or the vicar who
tries to persuade them that God is working in His own
mysterious way. The following speech occurs after a sticky
evening in which they have been visited both by their friends,
Freddie and Pam, and by Grace, Bri's mother. Grace insinu-
ates that Sheila is to blame for Joe's state of health, a punish-
ment for her promiscuous past. Here, Bri is talking directly
to the audience after Joe has been rushed into hospital. The
child has fallen into a coma as a result of Bri leaving her in
the back of his car in the freezing cold. Joe is recovering but
Bri is contemptuous of all talk of 'a lucky escape' and feels

that his marriage with Sheila has reached the end of the road.

Bri Sheila and I went with her in the ambulance. Mum stayed in Pam's car waiting for news. It was all-stations-go in the hospital – voluntary women rushing everywhere with soup and Bibles . . . St Bernards standing by . . .

Mimes hand-mike, assumes awe-stricken voice.

If there *is* anything heartening about such a disaster, I think it's the wonderful way this great operation of mercy has moved into action. And of course the uniquely British optimism that suddenly in moments of crisis seems to suffuse the whole nauseating atmosphere. I remember, when they first came in, the husband was jibbering and shaking like some spineless dago but nobody quite knew what to do. Then one of the impressive lesbian nurses pointed to the African orderlies and said quietly, 'Pull yourself together, man, set an example . . .'

Drops the parody.

Anyway the sawbones got to work with the oilcan and . . . 'I think there's a chance, Nurse . . . all our work may not be wasted . . .'

And the upshot was – finally Mum's feather fluttered.

He looks at the set, pausing for some seconds.

Sheila could hardly stand, what with anxiety and relief, so they gave her a bed for the night. Joe was staying in, of course, they couldn't say how long but perhaps a week.

I went in Freddie's car when he ran my mother back to the nunnery. She begged me to stay with her. 'I'll fill a nice hot-water bottle,' she said. And when I stood my ground,

'How about my electric blanket?' And I said, 'No, Mum. Cheerio, I'll be in touch,' and she started on about lighting the Valor stove that I loved so much because it threw patterns of light on the bedroom ceiling. I nearly choked with longing for that, but I gritted my teeth and said no, there was the budgie to be fed. And she said she had my old dummy and rattle somewhere . . . so in the end I ran . . . Freddie was a hoot. Saying it was a lucky escape and a blessing and stuff like that. His trouble, he's too kind-hearted, too squeamish. And he clings to law and order. Pam now. She's got the right idea. For the wrong reasons. Or something.

Look at me, delivering judgement. Who do you think you are – God? So – after they'd dropped me home – off they went to their three absolutely gorgeous kiddies – every one a company director – and the oil-fired heating – the labour-saving evergreens . . . the fibreglass yacht. I was glad to see the back of him. You can't think with that loudhailer going on and on. Not that there was *much* to think about. Only details.

Our marriage might have worked as well as most if Joe hadn't happened. I was too young for it, that's true, of course. I always will be. But Sheila might just have dragged me screaming into manhood. 'Stead of which, I was one of the menagerie. She loved me as much as any goldfish or aphelandra. So now it was a question of how to tell her I was leaving her. And when I went into it, I saw it wouldn't only be about Joe, but also my ambitions . . . and the first time I saw Father Christmas and – this backache's worse than yesterday and – the pattern on the ceiling . . . so in the end I better just creep away without a word . . .

Goes into room and begins hurriedly putting various objects into his pockets, putting on coat, etc.

So I've shaved and washed and packed a case . . .

[26]

Gets case from hall, stands it nearby.

Haven't decided where I'm going yet. Up the smoke, I suppose, get lost among the Australians.

Looks at watch.

Ordinary way I'd be leaving now for eyes-front-hands-on-heads . . . but never again, I tell you! Want a nice slow job . . . game-warden . . . keeper at Regent's Park . . . better still Kew Gardens . . .

Looks at room, his back to us, fixing it for ever.

Well.

Dogs Barking

RICHARD ZAJDLIC

*First produced at the Bush Theatre, London, in 1999 with
Tony Curran as Neil.*

Richard Zajdlic was one of the writers who contributed to
the cult television series *This Life*, depicting the sexual mores
of thirty-something London professionals. *Dogs Barking*
covers similar territory. Four months ago, Neil (early thirties) dumped Alex for his boss; the latter has since treated
him in a similar fashion, even, according to Neil, engineering
his dismissal. The play runs on rage as he returns to the one-
bedroom flat he once shared with Alex and demands to be
allowed to stay. She agrees that he can sleep on the sofa-bed
in the sitting room for a single night but, once inside, Neil
makes it clear that he has no intention of leaving. They are
typical Londoners in that when together they struggled to
get onto the first rung of the property ladder and Neil is
determined not to fall off. Although he made no contribution to the deposit, he has steadfastly refused to sign the flat
over to Alex and has now returned to claim his share. He
wants to take his revenge on women, to try to regain his male
pride. Far from grovelling to be allowed to return, he fights
dirty – stealing her stuff, her keys, and eventually trashing
the flat – although in the midst of this unpleasant battle there
are fleeting signs of an old affection. She meanwhile teases
him with the fact that she has acquired a new boyfriend, who
happens to be Neil's friend. Alex's sister tells Neil, 'You're
just something she stepped in. Still clinging to her shoes.'
Almost at the end of the play, Neil is sitting in the dark
surrounded by devastation. Alex has been taken to hospital
with a suspected miscarriage after Neil has hit her. His un-
lovely, timid friend Splodge returns to say that Alice and the

baby are both all right. Neil finally reveals the deeper feelings that lurk behind his aggression.

Neil What would *you* want? A totally, selfish, fucking wish. What do you want for you? (*Beat.*) I used to have this game with Alex. If you spotted an eyelash loose on their cheek, side of the nose – you'd gather it up, then hold it out for them to blow. Get a wish, see? We played it here that first night. She found one on me. Held it up. And I looked at her and thought . . . I wish this was enough. (*Beat.*) She used to say 'I love you' in a way that made me cringe. 'I love you, Neil' – in this whining, self-pitying tone that meant 'Don't leave me.' As though she knew, in her heart, that I wanted to go and that if she piled on enough emotional guilt maybe I wouldn't. And when I finally did I thought at least now I'll be free. At least now I won't ever hear that bleating tone again. But of course I did hear it again. Only it wasn't her saying it. It was me. 'I love you, Caroline.' 'Don't leave me.' (*Beat.*) I'd always had this arrogant sensibility that I deserved better – even leaving Alex was a kind of public declaration that I wasn't going to settle for second-rate. And here was Caroline making the same fucking declaration about me. It made me think that all those times when Alex said 'I love you,' maybe that's exactly what she meant. (*Beat.*) You'd better go.

East

STEVEN BERKOFF

*First produced at the Traverse Theatre, Edinburgh, by the
London Theatre Group in 1975 with Barry Philips as Les.*

This is an extremely popular audition piece, as is Steven
Berkoff's play, which is regularly revived, most especially at
the Edinburgh Festival. Berkoff in his introduction describes
the play 'as a revolt against the sloth of my youth and a
desire to turn a welter of undirected passion and frustration
into a positive form'. There is little plot. It's more a vivid
snapshot of working-class life in the East End described in a
series of speeches mostly spoken directly to the audience. Dad
reminisces affectionately about Oswald Mosely, the British
fascist leader; Mum wallows in TV and has an Oedipal
experience in the cinema; their son Mike and his friend Les
go on the razzle at the Lyceum, fight over Sylv, and run up
against the police.

   Berkoff has spent all his life fighting a battle against
realism and he has given very precise instructions as to how
East should be performed: 'The acting has to be loose and
smacking of danger . . . it must smart and whip out like a
fairy's wicked lash. There is no reserve and therefore no em-
barrassment.' The rhythmic torrent of language combined
with cockney slang demands a physical commitment as well
as a vocal one. The pent-up violence is poured into words
that often have a Shakespearean twist, and relish the London
place-names. In the following speech Les describes a trip on
the 38 bus from Holborn to Mount Pleasant. It's at first a
nostalgic account of London's past glories, but then plunges
into a no-holds-barred fantasy provoked by one of the classier
passengers.

Les Anyway I jumped on at Holborn and stood in that
recess where the clippie stands, when I saw the most awful
cracker. A right darlin' – I stood there clocking it, wanting
her to get the message, dulcet filthed, she was blonde with
medium-length hair, dyed straw but soft and straight and
her legs phenomenal. She had this short skirt on – and it
had tucked gently between her legs in case she flashed her
magic snare to some snatch bandit like me – and faces
jumped on and off never quite hiding my angel from me
but those legs with well-carved calves poured into some
very high thick-wedged shoes. She was a darlin' – I could
have breakfasted out of her knickers so sweetly pure she
was – I could have drunk the golden nectar from that
fountain, I could have loved her – wrapped her legs round
my throat, her bright arse trembling in my hands. Divine she
was and wore dark glasses but not so dark I couldn't see
that finest glint as she occasionally clocked me vardering
her like an ogre with a hard-on, ready to leap across the
bus and say darlin' climb aboard this, but she was almost
too perfect. I stood all the way – unable to leave, like a
sentinel at the post and my lover was there – and I thought,
Mike, I thought of Doris and I thought of all the fat
scrubbers I get with soggy tits – I thought of all those dirty
scrubbers and how, just once in my life, I'd like to walk
down the street with that. Why don't we chat up classy
snatch? Why is it that we pull slags? We pull what we think
we are, Mike – it tumbled then – it dropped – the dirty
penny – that we get what we ARE. What we think we are,
so when we have a right and merry laugh with some
unsavoury bunk-up or gang-bang behind the Essoldo we
are doing it to ourselves. We are giving ourselves what we

deserve. It came to me then – here it was, the most delectable
snatch in the world REAL with those INCREDIBLE pins and
CLEAN – and then she stirred just ever so little it was but
she knew I was lapping it up – and she uncrossed her legs
to get up. She was going but maybe my wires got through
to her and she thought why not give that geezer – he's not a
bad-looking bloke – a flash and as she uncrossed her DIVINE
THIGHS I swivelled my sockets up there and some creep
moved right in front of her but I just caught the slightest
glimpse of heaven – the clouds passed over the sun but it
reappeared again – she stood up on the platform waiting
to leap off at Farringdon Road with that thin skirt on –
a thin black cotton skirt – God she must have known that
the sun pours through that skirt – no slip, just her AMAZING
FUCKING FORM. Up to the ARSE. Like she was naked,
standing there waiting for the bus to stop at Mount Pleasant
where she jumped off – and I wanted to jump off, Mike –
I wanted to get off the bus and run after her – but what
could I say – she strode down the street – strong on these
DELIRIOUS PEGS with those nasty post-office workers
leering her beautiful form with their dim and faded jellies
and I couldn't get off the bus – I didn't have the guts – I
didn't know what to say to her, Mike! What words could
my gob sprach?! And then I saw her cross into Clerkenwell
Road, when she disappeared.

Faith Healer

BRIAN FRIEL

*First produced at the Longacre Theatre, New York, in 1979
with James Mason as Frank.*

Truth is slippery in Brian Friel's great play *Faith Healer*.
Three characters – Frank Hardy; Grace, who is his mistress
or possibly his wife; and Teddy, his cockney manager – speak
four monologues giving their differing versions of their life
together on the road. Frank Hardy – the initials are appro-
priate – is tormented with the elusive gift of healing. Like a
neurotic artist he is always haunted by the possibility of his
talent deserting him. His preoccupation with his gift makes
it impossible for him to give himself to another person. Frank
is not a con man. They are all agreed that in a small church
hall in Wales he cured ten people. But the gift is not reliable
and increasingly eludes him as he takes more and more to
the bottle. If the facts are elusive, Friel gives a very precise
description of Frank, even down to his vivid green socks. He
is middle-aged, grey or greying, with a pale, lined face. He is
dressed in a shabby overcoat with the collar up at the back.
In Frank's first monologue, he describes how he returns home
to Ireland after getting the news in Kinlochbervie, Scotland,
that his mother has had a heart attack. Later we learn that
Kinlochbervie is the place where, abandoned by Frank,
Grace gave birth in the back of the van and buried their dead
baby. As Frank describes his homecoming, you can feel his
anxiety as he looks down at his mother and wonders initially
whether he will be able to cure her, before his father reveals
that she has died shortly before he arrived. The incantation
of place names is important to Frank. He believes that it
helps him to calm his nerves before what he teasingly describes as a performance.

Frank We were in the north of Scotland when I got word that my mother had had a heart attack. In a village called Kinlochbervie, in Sutherland, about as far north as you can go in Scotland. A picturesque little place, very quiet, very beautiful, looking across to the Isle of Lewis in the Outer Hebrides; and we were enjoying a few days' rest there. Anyhow, when the news came, Teddy drove me down to Glasgow. Gracie wanted to come with me and couldn't understand when I wouldn't take her. But she used her incomprehension as fuel for her loyalty and sent me off with a patient smile.

It was my first time home in twenty years. My father had retired and was living in a housing estate outside Dublin. When he opened the door he didn't recognise me – I had to tell him who I was. Then he shook my hand as if I were an acquaintance and led me up to the bedroom.

She was exactly as I remembered her – illness hadn't ravaged her. Sleeping silently. Her skin smooth and girlish, her chin raised as if in expectation. Jesus, I thought, O my Jesus, what am I going to do?

'She looks nice,' he said.

'Yes,' I said. 'She looks great.'

He cleared his throat.

'She passed away quietly. You missed her by approximately one hour and ten minutes,' as if he were giving evidence. And then he cried.

And I felt such overwhelming relief that when he cried, I cried easily with him.

Twelve years later I was back in Ireland again; with Teddy and Gracie. Things had been lean for a long time. Or as Teddy put it, 'If we want to eat, we've got to open up new

territory, dear 'eart. You've cured 'em all 'ere. Come on –
let's go to the lush pickings of Ireland.' And I agreed
because I was as heartsick of Wales and Scotland as they
were. And the whiskey wasn't as efficient with the questions
as it had been. And my father had died in the meantime. And
I suppose because I always knew we would end up there.
So on the last day of August we crossed from Stranraer to
Larne and drove through the night to County Donegal. And
there we got lodgings in a pub, a lounge bar, really, outside
a village called Ballybeg, not far from Donegal Town.

There was no sense of homecoming. I tried to simulate it
but nothing stirred. Only a few memories, wan and neutral.
One of my father watching me through the bars of the day-
room window as I left for school – we lived in a rented
house across the street. One of playing with handcuffs,
slipping my hands in and out through the rings. One of
my mother making bread and singing a hymn to herself.
'Yes, heaven, yes, heaven, yes, heaven is the prize.' And one
of a group of men being shown over the barracks – I think
they were inspectors from Dublin – and my father saying,
'Certainly, gentlemen, by all means, gentlemen, anything
you say, gentlemen.' Maybe one or two other memories.
They evoked nothing.

Frozen

BRYONY LAVERY

*First produced at the Birmingham Repertory Theatre in
1998, then at the National Theatre, London, with Tom
Georgeson as Ralph.*

Playwright Bryony Lavery deals with the almost unbearable
subject of the abuse and murder of a child but scrupulously
manages to avoid either sensationalism or sentimentality. Her
integrity is never in question. *Frozen* has a cast of just three
characters, who speak as much to the audience as they do to
each other: Nancy, who sends her ten-year-old daughter Rhona
round to her grandma's with a pair of secateurs and never sees
her again; Agnetha, the American psychiatrist who is explor-
ing the theory that child abuse causes profound and patholo-
gical changes in the structure of the brain as surely as injury
does; and Ralph, the serial killer who only cares for his tattoos
and his secret collection of videos, with titles such as *Lollitots*,
and *Lesbian Lolita*.

Twenty years after Rhona disappears, Ralph is caught and
it is Agnetha's job to interrogate him. It quickly becomes clear
that he provides further proof for her theory, in particular that
abused children lack the ability to make emotional bonds,
that their brains actually look different from those with happier backgrounds. Ralph shows no remorse at all; all he
worries about is that killing girls isn't legal. He fantasises
about a childhood in which he was 'spoilt rotten' and his
parents sat around reading poetry. To Nancy, however, he
describes a father who washed his mouth out with soap and
water and beat him on the side of his head. Forced by Nancy
to recognise what he has done, he is unable to cope and
commits suicide.

This speech, however, is the first that he makes to the audience in which he chillingly describes how he lured Rhona into the van. He is an isolated obsessive, and the title *Frozen* applies as much to him as it does to Agnetha and Nancy.

Ralph, in his own room, washing his hands at a sink.

Ralph
You know

it's one of those days
you're just going to do it
you might do it.
I suppose mostly I'm a bit of a cold fish.

He dries his hands carefully on a small, clean towel.

But then, these times
things hot up.
It's been a bit of a bad patch for me . . .
fucking landlady . . .
pardon my French . . .
despite I told her I don't eat lamb . . .
despite I told her I'm not a big eater . . .
despite I made that clear . . .
turns up on the plate
and I've eaten it before I've said
'This isn't lamb is it . . .?'
and it *was* . . .

Takes a small bottle of hand lotion, pours a dollop on one palm, starts to rub it into both hands.

And I've gone out with
hoojit . . . Raymond Quantock . . .
and that wassname from work . . . Dick Bottle . . .
and I've kept up with them putting it away . . .
otherwise . . .
and drunk five lager tops

and two . . . (*Counts in his head.*) . . . four . . .
Jack Daniels
and I've gone over on that damn foot again . . .
lightning strike of pain . . .
and it's put me in a strop
nobody better mess with me
nobody better
been like . . . offish
and . . .

He's on a street somewhere.

I just see her
and decide
I'm going to get her in the van.
I just want to keep her for a bit
spend some time with her.
I just do it.
It's a rush of blood.
Hello.

I said 'Hello'
are you deaf?
It's rude to ignore people.
Are you loony?
You're loony.
I'm only being polite.
No need to get the hump.
Not with me.
I just said 'Hello.'
Hello.
Hello.
Hello.
I'm saying 'Hello' to you.
Least you can do is make conversation.
Kind of world is this
folk can't be sociable?

Polite.
Least you can do is make a response.
It's Bad Manners if you don't.
Bad manners.
Rude.
I said 'Hello.'
Hello.
Hello.
Hello.
Hello.
Hello then . . .
finally . . .
finally . . .
she goes
'Hello.'

I think she quite liked me.

Oh yes
she was interested.

The van's down here
obviously
the back door's not locked
because I've thought ahead
obviously
she wants to come
it's only fifty yards
it's convenient.

I've got cushions in the back
And a sleeping bag.
Obviously.

Sometimes you're fucked by
circumstances
things don't go your way.

Picks something up. Regards it.

The secateurs
I don't bargain for
but
in the event
they turn out
useful
and add to it all
passing off
efficiently
but
logistically
she's persuaded it's time
to get in the van
you make it work
she's in the van.

A sound of deliberate snipping of plants . . .
  He puts the top on the bottle of hand lotion. Secures it.

Lovely evening.
Sunny . . . but with a light southerly breeze . . .

Gagarin Way

GREGORY BURKE

*First produced at the Traverse Theatre, Edinburgh, in 2001
with Michael Nardone as Eddie, then transferred to the
National Theatre, London, in the same year.*

The play's title – *Gagarin Way* – derives from a street in Lum-
phinnans, an area of Fife in Scotland that was once a hotbed
of communism. Today the mines have gone, the redundant
miners have only their memories, and the younger genera-
tion works either in internationally owned factories, in call
centres, or in the service economy. This mix of political thril-
ler and explosive comedy is driven by Eddie, a loose cannon
in his early thirties, who teams up with the more traditional
left-winger Gary to carry out a cock-eyed plan. Their idea is
to seize one of the Japanese managers of the factory in which
they work and kill him. This is their revenge on the global-
ised economy. The play is set at night in a storeroom, and begins with a riotous conversation about Sartre and Genet in
which Eddie runs rings round Tom, the graduate security
guard whose misfortune it is to get mixed up in this heist.
Tom likes to pick and mix aspects of socialism and capital-
ism that appeal to him; Eddie is more extreme, and the unnerving speech that follows is an indication of just how wild
he can be. Subsequently the abduction goes disastrously
wrong, including the discovery that their hostage, Frank,
comes from Fife rather than Osaka and is so world-weary
he has no desire to defend either his own or the company's
actions. His cynicism is in complete contrast with Eddie's
driving, dangerous energy. Quentin Tarantino's influence is
felt in the mix of violence and comedy, especially in Eddie's
ludicrous failure to wear a balaclava and hide his identity
because he's allergic to wool.

[47]

At this point in the play, Frank is still flat out after being hit on the head, and Tom has discovered that Gary and Eddie are into something rather more serious than the thieving he was bribed to turn a blind eye to at the beginning. Eddie appears to want to reassure Tom, but the following explanation does more to wind him up.

Eddie (*to Tom*) It's no big deal. You can day anything now ay. Anything. Unlimited lifestyle choice. Whatever you want tay day in your spare time . . . you can day it. (*Beat.*) I've never been a political person. No till now. But I've always been interested in violence. Always . . . ken . . . really enjoyed it. (*Beat.*) I tried all the gratuitous stuff, the recreational violence ken, the leathering folk just for the sheer, amoral pleasure ay leathering them . . . and it was good at the time, dinnay get me wrong . . . but . . . ken the law ay diminishing marginal returns . . . it always kicks in eventually ay. (*Beat.*) Too many dysfunctional cunts involved tay ay. Too many cunts way problems. (*Beat.*) I thought . . . seen as how I'm a bit more mature now, seen as how I've advanced way beyond the point ay thinking going home to kick the loved ones in the puss is the path tay spiritual contentment, I thought I should maybe try something more idealistic, something way a point . . . see if that's what I needed. Ken . . . it's maybe more satisfying . . . violence way a reason. (*Beat.*) Gary here (*indicates Gary*) . . . he's always been a wee bit ay a political animal. We thought we'd put the two together and see if they still had a contribution tay make tay the modern workplace.

The Hothouse

HAROLD PINTER

*First produced at Hampstead Theatre, London, in 1980
with Derek Newark as Roote, then transferred to the
Ambassadors Theatre in the same year.*

Harold Pinter wrote *The Hothouse* in 1958 and then put it
away in the wake of the bad reviews that *The Birthday Party*
received in London. He didn't bring it out again until 1980,
when it was staged at Hampstead. The play then re-emerged
in 1995 in a transfer from Chichester to the West End, with
Pinter distinguishing himself as Roote, the spluttering boss
of what is euphemistically known as a 'rest home'. More terri-
fying versions of this place feature in Pinter's later, more overtly
political plays, *One for the Road* and *Mountain Language*.

A dangerous combination of megalomania and incompe-
tence, Roote is cracking under the strain as he tries to keep a
tight control over his patients, who are known by numbers
rather than names. He enquires with clenched-teeth menace
after their welfare. He attempts to be tough on his staff too,
aggressively demanding at one point to know whether his
deputy Gibbs is 'taking the old wee-wee'.

Early on in the play, Roote is appalled to discover from
Gibbs that one patient has died and another given birth. His
dismay is all to do with the threat to the institution and
nothing to do with the plight of the patients. This speech is
a typical example of Roote's indignant bluster, as he tries,
like any conservative, to summon up the forces of tradition
to help reassert his authority. Shortly afterwards it becomes
obvious, in an extended music-hall joke, that Roote is the
father of the baby.

Roote This has made my morning. It really has made my morning.

He takes a pair of glasses out of his pocket, puts them on and looks across the room to Gibbs.

I'm dumbstruck. Quite thunderstruck. Absolutely thunder-struck! This has never happened before. Never! In all the years I've been here, in all the years my predecessor was here. And I'm quite certain never before him. To spend years and years, winter after winter, trying to perfect the working of an institution so fragile in its conception and execution, so fragile the boundary between the achievement of one's aspirations and their collapse, not only one's own aspirations; rather the aspirations of a whole community, a tradition, an ideal; such a delicately wrought concept of participation between him who is to be treated and him who is to treat that it defies analysis; trying to sustain this fine, fine balance, finer than a . . . finer than a . . . far, far finer. Year after year, and so refined the operation that the softest breath, the breath of a . . . feather. . . can send the whole thing tottering into chaos, into ignominy, to the death and cancellation of all our hopes. Goodness gracious.

He stands.

As my predecessor said, on one unforgettable occasion: 'Order, gentlemen, for God's sake, order!' I remember the silence, row upon row of electrified faces, he with his golden forelock, his briar burning, upright and commanding, a soldier's stance, looking down from the platform. The gymnasium was packed to suffocation, standing room only. The lucky ones were perched on vaulting horses, hanging without movement from the wallbars. 'Order, gentlemen,' he said, 'for the love of Mike!' As one man we looked out of the window at Mike, and gazed at the statue – covered in snow, it so happened, then as now. Mike! The predecessor of my predecessor, the predecessor of us all, the man who laid the foundation stone, the man who introduced the first patient, the man who, after the incredible hordes of patients, or would-be patients, had followed him through town and country, hills and valleys, waited under hedges, lined the bridges and sat six feet deep in the ditch, opened institution after institution up and down the country, rest homes, nursing homes, convalescent homes, sanatoria. He was sanctioned by the Ministry, revered by the populace, subsidised by the State. He had set in motion an activity for humanity, of humanity and by humanity. And the keyword was order.

He turns to Gibbs.

I, Gibbs, have tried to preserve that order. A vocation, in fact. And you choose Christmas morning to come and tell me this. I tell you quite frankly I smell disaster.

Howard Katz

PATRICK MARBER

*First produced at the National Theatre, London, in 2001
with Ron Cook as Howard Katz.*

Howard Katz is a Jewish agent who represents a motley
collection of celebrities. At fifty, he is tearing his life apart,
challenging the God he doesn't believe in to give him per-
sonal proof that there is a reason to live. The play begins on
a park bench as Katz contemplates suicide, and effectively
takes place in flashback. He represents those involved in the
tackier end of showbiz and has always been abrasive. His
brother says of him: 'You sold your soul so long ago you
don't remember the *price*.' Nor does he do anything to hide
his contempt for his clients, shouting at one 'artiste' who has
had rather too much plastic surgery that she looks like 'a
skull on a stick'. Not surprisingly, as a stream of clients head
for the door, his partners get concerned and here suggest that
he takes what they euphemistically describe as a break. Although Katz despises his job, their suggestion causes him to
panic and provokes a typically aggressive response. Katz's
marriage has already fallen apart, and his father has died
after a row they never resolved.

There are further depths to go as he loses his job, throws
his money away – recklessly losing it at a casino – and ends
up on the street. Back on the park bench, he finally emerges
from his nightmare, and through the memory of his son's
birth once more feels connected to the rest of the human race.
It's an unusually uplifting conclusion for playwright Patrick
Marber. Unlike his other plays, it didn't transfer to the West
End, but it's hard to forget its mix of rancour and wit.

Katz Do you know how much commission I bring in?
I'm doing all right – and I'm not saying I'm so *great* or
anything but – *Jesus* – I look after all the flotsam and
jetsam nobody *wants*: the weather girls and the chefs
and the gardeners and the game-show winners, the singers
who want to act and the actors who want to sing, strange
blonde ladies with one name. I've got a client in the *Scrubs* –
I visit him once a month. Alcoholics, cokeheads, perverts,
the lost and the mad – 'Sling 'em down the corridor to
Howard, he'll mop up.' Hideous, *hideous* egos – all of
them – *monsters* – kicking and screaming for their 'fifteen
minutes' – and on top of that I'm brown-nosing the press
and sucking up to ad-men and gobbling off the broadcasters
and milking the tits of every vicious, fame-fucking publicist
in London – it's *Sodom* and *Gomorrah* out there – but
without the *scenery* – and I'm squelching around in this . . .
this infantile morass, holding the clients' hands and wiping
their chins through every piddling 'crisis' in their so-called
'lives' and I'm doing this 24/7 for YOU. I am *Juggling
Turds* Every Day Of My *Life* so that this *noble* agency can
look after the so called 'artists' who don't actually earn us
enough *commission* TO PAY THE RENT ON THE OFFICE.

Luther

JOHN OSBORNE

*First produced at the Theatre Royal, Nottingham, by the
English Stage Company in 1961 with Julian Glover as the
Knight.*

Contemporary critics were puzzled by Osborne's choice of a
historical subject when he had previously done so much to
pin down their own times. It could have had something to do
with the influence of Bertolt Brecht's *Galileo*, but the critic
Kenneth Tynan suggests that John Osborne was attracted to
the subject of Luther, the sixteenth-century religious leader,
both because of Luther's resistance to authority and because
of the way in which he was hailed as a popular hero by people
whose causes he neither approved of nor shared. In a similar
fashion, Osborne was acclaimed as a leader of the social
revolution in the late fifties – he reluctantly took part in a
CND demonstration and was arrested for civil disobedience –
when he was really far more of an individualist, even emerg-
ing later as a traditionalist.

  This speech by the Knight, one of Luther's followers, comes
immediately after a scene in which Martin Luther triumphs
at the Diet of Worms in 1521 and refuses to bow down to
papal authority. The Knight reflects on what it felt like to
hear the powerful words pouring out of such an obviously
sick body – Luther suffered terribly from constipation – and
how he then believed that the world would never be the
same again. Four years have passed and disillusionment has
now set in. At his feet lies the body of a peasant. It's not entirely clear in the text, but Luther controversially took a stand
against these peasants when, as well as supporting the preacher
in his spiritual demands, they also called for freedom from
the despotism of the political authorities. Their uprising was

defeated with Luther's help in 1525. Here the corpse is a reminder of the bloody events that followed. The battle-weary Knight resents Luther's support for the aristocrats.

Knight There was excitement that day. In Worms – that
day I mean. Oh, I don't mean now, not now. A lot's
happened since then. There's no excitement like that any
more. Not unless murder's your idea of excitement. I tell
you, you can't have ever known the kind of thrill that
monk set off amongst that collection of all kinds of men
gathered together there – those few years ago. We all felt it,
every one of us, just without any exception, you couldn't
help it, even if you didn't want to, and, believe me, most of
those people didn't want to. His scalp looked blotchy and
itchy, and you felt sure, just looking at him, his body must
be permanently sour and white all over, even whiter than
his face and like a millstone to touch. He'd sweated so
much by the time he'd finished, I could smell every inch of
him even from where I was. But he fizzed like a hot spark
in a trail of gunpowder going off in us, that dowdy monk,
he went off in us, and nothing could stop it, and it blew up
and there was nothing we could do, any of us, that was it.
I just felt quite sure, quite certain in my own mind nothing
could ever be the same again, just simply that. Something
had taken place, something had changed and become
something else, an event had occurred in the flesh, in the
flesh and the breath – like, even like when the weight of
that body slumped on its wooden crotch-piece and the
earth grew dark. That's the kind of thing I mean by happen,
and this also happened in very likely the same manner to
all those of us who stood there, friends and enemies alike.
I don't think, no, I don't think even if I could speak and
write like him, I could begin to give you an idea of what
we thought, or what some of us thought, of what we might

come to. Obviously, we couldn't have all felt quite the same way, but I wanted to burst my ears with shouting and draw my sword – no, not draw it, I wanted to pluck it as if it were a flower in my blood and plunge it into whatever he would have told me to.

The Knight is lost in his own thoughts, then his eyes catch the body of the peasant. He takes a swipe at the cart.

If one could only understand him. He baffles me, I just can't make him out. Anyway, it never worked out. (*To corpse.*) Did it, my friend? Not the way we expected anyway, certainly not the way *you* expected, but who'd have ever thought we might end up on different sides, him on one and us on the other. That when the war came between you and them, he'd be there beating the drum for *them* outside the slaughterhouse, and beating it louder and better than anyone, hollering for *your* blood, cutting you up in your thousands, and hanging you up to drip away into the fire for good. Oh well, I suppose all those various groups were out for their different things, or the same thing really, all out for what we could get, and more than any of us had the right to expect.

Man of the Moment

ALAN AYCKBOURN

*First produced at the Stephen Joseph Theatre in the Round,
Scarborough, in 1988 with Jon Strickland as Douglas.
Transferred to the Globe Theatre, London, with Michael
Gambon as Douglas in 1990.*

There's no getting away from the fact that Douglas is a bit of
a nerd. Jill, the television reporter, certainly thinks so. In
Alan Ayckbourn's *Man of the Moment*, Jill is in Spain bring-
ing together two men – anticipating by some years the current
vogue for reality TV – whose lives first clashed seventeen years
ago. Vic was robbing a bank when Douglas, a weedy bank
clerk, tried to stop him by seizing his shotgun. In the struggle
the gun went off, hitting another staff member, Nerys, in the
face. She is now Douglas's wife. He had always admired her
from afar, but before her injuries she was out of his reach,
invariably pursued by more desirable, handsome men than
he. Vic has done his time – nine years – but since then has become a media star and has moved to a luxurious Spanish villa
on the proceeds with Trudy, his unhappy, beautiful wife.
Douglas's bravery, on the other hand, doesn't rate on the celeb-
rity Richter scale. Jill describes him as being about as 'lively
as a sheet of laminated chipboard'. Later she says: 'It's not
that he won't talk. You can usually cope with that . . . But
this man, he's deadly. The point is, there's absolutely nothing
you can say to him that he doesn't agree with. He smothers
you with approval. It's like interviewing a fire blanket.'

Here Douglas confesses things to Trudy that he could
never tell Jill, most especially why he feels fortunate in spite
of his obscurity, Nerys's injuries, and their lack of money.
Later, he shows that he has not lost his impetuosity when
faced with a bully.

[63]

Douglas She liked me. And more important, she needed me. That's what mattered. And I loved her. (*He smiles.*) I was going to tell you, you know, when I'd left the bank, I applied for my present job with this double-glazing company. I thought it might – you know – increase my standing with her. Since she seemed to have a liking for double-glazing men. Ridiculous. We laughed about that later. I never regretted it, though. They're a grand bunch. Anyway, she came out. And we married quietly. And we got a joint mortgage on number fifty-three and we've lived there ever since. With never a cross word, I'm happy to report. (*Pause.*) So what do I say? Yes, I do – I hate Vic because of what he did to the most beautiful woman in the world? Or, thank you very much, Vic, for being instrumental in arranging for me to marry the unattainable girl of my dreams? Difficult to know which to say, isn't it? (*Pause.*) All right. I know you might well say, what about her? What about poor old Nerys? Being forced to settle for minor league when she was naturally first division. Well, all I can say is, without prejudice, and I am not a swearing person, you appreciate – but that man she was engaged to originally – old double-glazing the first – he was a complete – pillock. He really was. He treated Nerys like – well, there were times when – not just me, you understand . . . We all could have done – in that bank. Including Mr Marsh. This man – he treated her as only a handsome man can treat a beautiful woman. If you know what I mean.

The Mercy Seat

NEIL LABUTE

First produced at the Manhattan Class Company (MCC) Theater, New York City in 2002 with Liev Schreiber as Ben Harcourt.

Although the setting of Neil LaBute's play is described vaguely as 'New York City, not long ago', in fact, it becomes instantly clear that 11 September 2001 is a very recent event. For a start, there is a layer of dust that covers the furniture in Abby's spacious loft apartment and an amber haze can be seen outside the window. Ben, described as 'maybe thirty-three', is sitting with his ringing cellphone unanswered on his lap when Abby walks in. It emerges that if he had not stopped off at Abby's apartment to have sex with her, he would almost certainly have been one of the terrorists' victims. Abby is not only twelve years older but also his boss, and if that didn't make their relationship sufficiently complicated, Ben is married with children. Disasters can bring out the best in people, but he is consumed with the opportunity that the attack has provided to change his life. Given that nobody knows where he is, he could join the list of those killed, disappear with Abby and start again. Most of all, he would never have to find the courage to sit down with his wife and tell her that he wanted a divorce. He would also, as Abby points out, never be able to see his children again, a sacrifice he seems prepared to make.

It's hardly surprising that Abby is sceptical about the scheme and taken aback by Ben's response to a national tragedy. It provokes a long night of the soul in which they pick their relationship apart. The way they have sex and their behaviour at work comes under the spotlight. Ben feels diminished by Abby's sense of humour and her use of cultural references that are unfamiliar to him. She dislikes his secrecy about his family. As much as she would like to spend her life with Ben, she can't be comfortable with the man sitting in front of her, failing to ring his wife to say that he's all right, and apparently also failing to take in the scale of what is happening outside. They reminisce about happier times in the past. 'Back,' Abby crisply states, 'when we liked each other.' In the speech that follows, Ben attempts to explain himself.

Ben Jesus. . . you think I was born this way, like some cut-throat *pirate* of the high seas? Huh? Hell, I'm just trying to muddle through, that's all, just muddle my fucking way through to middle age, see if I can make it that far. You like trivia so goddamn much, well, here's a little tidbit for ya . . . I'm *faking* it. OK? Totally getting by on fumes. I put my *game* face on and go out there and I'm scared shitless. (*Beat.*) You know what? I take that back . . . This *is* me. I've screwed up every step of my life, Abby, I'm not afraid to admit it. Happy to, actually, I am happy to sing it out there for anybody who wants to hear. I always take the easy route, do it faster, simpler, you know, whatever it takes to get it done, be liked, get by. That's me. Cheated in school, screwed over my friends, took whatever I could get from whomever I could take it from. My marriage, there's a goddamn fiasco, of which you're intimately aware. The kids . . . I barely register as a dad, I'm sure, but compared to the other shit in my life, I'm Doctor-fucking-*Spock*. No matter what I do or have done, they adore the hell out of me, and I'm totally knocked out by that. What kids are like. Yeah. (*Beat.*) And you, let's not forget you. *Us.* OK, yes, I haven't done all that I've promised, said I'd do, I fuck up along the way. All right. But I'm trying, this time out – with you, I mean – I have been trying. Don't know what it looks like, feels to you, but I have made a real go of us, and that is not a lie. It isn't. And so then, yesterday . . . through all the smoke and fear and just, I dunno, *apocalyptic* shit . . . I see a way for us to go for it, to totally erase the past – and I don't think it makes me Lucifer or a criminal or some bad man because I noticed it. I really don't. We've been given something here. A chance to . . . I don't know what, to wash

away a lot of the, just, rotten crap we've done. More than
anything else, that's what this is. A chance. I know it is.

Moon on a Rainbow Shawl

ERROL JOHN

*First produced in a revised version at the East 11th Street
Theatre, New York, in 1962 with James Earl Jones as
Ephraim.*

In 1956, the actor, Errol John won an *Observer* playwriting
prize with *Moon on a Rainbow Shawl*, which was then first
produced at the Royal Court, London, in 1958 before a revised
version was staged in New York. All the characters in John's
atmospheric play dream of escaping the crowded, dilapi-
dated backyard in Trinidad where they live just after the
Second World War. Sophia is the hard-working, sharp-eyed
matriarch who scorns their greedy landlord. Her husband
Charlie is a defeated man – once a talented cricket player
who refused to kowtow to the establishment, now reduced
to mending bats for the local rich boys. When their daughter
wins a scholarship to a good school (an unusual note of
optimism in the play), Charlie foolishly steals from the landlord's café in order to pay for her uniform. Sophia fights with
Mavis, a young floozie who brings paying customers, mostly
US soldiers, back to her room for sex.

Of them all, Ephraim, a trolley-bus driver, is the most determined to escape not only the yard, but also Trinidad. It's a
demanding part for a young black actor. He has somehow
managed to save enough money to emigrate to Liverpool,
where he imagines that there will be plenty of opportunities
for a man like him. That's unfortunate for Rosa, who also
lives in the yard. She loves Ephraim and is trying to avoid the
attentions of their landlord. Throughout the play, Ephraim is
under pressure from others and his own conscience to give
up his dream: to lend Sophia and Charlie money for bail when
Charlie gets caught; but most of all to marry Rosa and become

a bus inspector. Here, Rosa has just told him that she's pregnant. He thinks it's a trick to trap him and he tells her this story to prove how ruthless he can be.

Ephraim Rosa. Rose. Rose – don't shed no tears for me –
I was never worth that kind of water. Rosa – listen to me!
Look! Look!

*He has taken a framed photograph from his trunk.
Kneeling beside the girl, he pulls her to him.*

Yer see this picture of ole Grandma here? . . . She took care
of me from the time I small – till I grow a man! My ole
man died when I was five years old. When I was six – my
mother pick up with another man – went off to Curaçao! –
and left me flat! For nearly a whole week I went hungry –
till Grandma came and found me and took me home with
her. So it was only me and Gram from all that time . . .
Then come a time. I began to make my plans. I find that she
was in my way. I wanted to save money ! – But she was in
my way. So one day – I went to her – told her – I was putting
her in the poor house . . . Four days – after I took her there –
she died. . . .

He has told his story without any display of emotion.

When they knew she was dying. They send and call me.
She was lying there on the bed. I couldn't believe it was she.
In four days – she had sort of – wasted away. I stood up by
the door – I couldn't go no farther. She was looking at me.
But I just stood there. Shame! eating me! . . . I heard her
ask the nurse for me to come near. Perhaps – to forgive me –
I don't know. But I couldn't go. I couldn't go. Then she told
the nurse: Tell that boy if he can't come nearer – he might
as well go! . . . She died that night. . . .

Rosa moves to console him.

(*Pulling away.*) DON'T TOUCH ME! So don't think – don't think a little trap like you could ketch me – just by sayin' yer going to have a baby fer mey. When that boat-whistle blow! – It mean I leaving all this behind! This picture!

He throws the frame spinning to the floor.

You and Ole Mack! Charlie! Mrs Adams! Esther! – The whole damn blasted lot! . . .

Listen to me, Rosa! I got a life to live! Awright! So I stay here. I come an inspector on the trolley. To what end? Turn macco like the rest. Stand at a bus stop. Hop on the trolley. Check the tickets. Hop off the trolley! To what end, Rosa? Just so as to see the conductors don't rob the blasted City Corporation? . . .

That is not for me! Outside somewhere in the world I feel for certain sure it got more for me than that!

Night of the Soul

DAVID FARR

*First produced in The Pit at the Barbican Centre, London,
by the Royal Shakespeare Company in 2002 with Tom
Mannion as Francis.*

David Farr's *Night of the Soul* is a play about reconciliation
and forgiveness and the effect of the past on the present,
improbably illustrated by the relationship between a six-
hundred-year-old ghost and a forty-year-old consultant in
market research. Tom Mannion played Francis, the man with
a guilty secret, who describes what he does as 'an empty
fucking job for empty fucking people'. The ghost, who meets
Francis in the hotel she haunts, needs him to seek reconciliation in order for her to be released from purgatory. Over all
these years, he is only the second person who has been able
to see her.

Francis spends his life on the road, earning vast sums of
money, rarely seeing his son, and barely caring that his wife
is having an affair. All feeling died in him eighteen years ago
when he had a terrible row with his father, an ex-docker, laid
off because of his back, who believed in the community
values that his ambitious son has rejected. During the row,
Francis refuses to engage with his father's worries but rather
tries to pay his way out of his responsibilities. When the
money is rejected, Francis is so frustrated that he bashes his
parents' dog to death, leaving someone else to take the blame.
He has not visited the childhood home since. His devoted
mother, unaware of what really happened, has always blamed
her husband for Francis's absence. Before the play starts, she
rings, begging him to see his father and make his peace with
him before he dies. Francis ignores the message. Here, in the
middle of one of his training sessions, his phone goes off and

he discovers he's left it too late. The strength of his reaction contrasts with the comedy of the session that precedes it.

Francis Hi. I'm Francis Chappell. Thanks for coming.
I know you've all got busy lives to lead so I'll try to make
these two hours worthwhile. (*off mike*) That's how I always
start. Nice and relaxed. Make them feel at home. Play a
little game to warm them up. I've been doing this half my
life, I know a few tricks. That day was no different. I
played the game. (*on mike*) Separate into pairs. You don't
need to move. Just find someone you've never met before.
That's very important. Have we all found someone? Sir?
Great. Now look at them and let them look at you too.
Don't be embarrassed. Nothing strange is going to happen.
You won't have to kiss them. Look at their face, their
clothes. Look in their eyes. Start to make some hunches
about this person. Who are they? Where are they from?
What do they do? How old are they? Are they with
someone else here? Are they alone? Are they from a
discernible social class? How do they vote? What religion
are they? What sexual orientation? Do they smoke? Do
they cook? Do they come here often? You're a detective,
and you're searching for clues to the state of mind and
body of this person.

   Two minutes. And you've started to paint your picture.
Now decide. What is it above anything else that this person
wants? Could be a haircut. Could be a holiday. Could be
great sex. A lasting and fulfilling relationship with someone
who *really* understands them. A new mortgage? A new job?
A new heart?

   Make a decision. One thing you would give them if you
could. Now tell them what it is. They won't reply. You will
never know if you were right. Tell them now.

   OK, you can relax.

What you've just done is a very simple piece of intuitive market research.

It is the dream of every company, every political party, every consumer group and polling organisation, to do what you've just done: to climb inside someone's head and find out what that person really wants.

Francis's beeper vibrates.

Sorry about this, I normally turn it off but I have some news coming from Leeds. (*He reads the message.*) And that isn't it. (*He laughs.*) Where was I? The dial. If you all look at the back of the seat in front of you, you'll see a dial. This is your love/loathe dial. I'm going to show you a film. I want you to react to every image you see. If you love it, turn it one way, if you hate it, turn it the other.

Francis's beeper vibrates again.

I'm really sorry. (*He reads the message.*) My wife. Again. (*He laughs. Beat.*) So: the love/loathe dial.

The beeper vibrates again. Francis looks at it again. It is clearly the same message.

Excuse me, I just have to sort this out.

He calls on his mobile aware that the audience is listening in.

Hi, it's me. Listen, I'm in the middle of a session, can I call you back? I know it's on, it's on in case Leeds call. (*Beat.*) Can't it wait? No, listen, I'll call you back. I said I'll call you back. (*Beat.*) What is so important?

Pause. Francis listens, drops the mike, then suddenly sits down on the floor.

OK. I think the best thing to do now. (*Beat. He takes the mike.*) What I normally like to do at this stage. (*Beat. Into the mike*) My father's dead.

The Old Country

ALAN BENNETT

*First produced at the Queen's Theatre, London, in 1977
with Alec Guinness as Hilary.*

This is one of three plays about upper-class spies written by
Alan Bennett, the others being *An Englishman Abroad* and
A Question of Attribution. Most people assumed when the
play first opened that Hilary was based on Kim Philby, although Bennett denies it in the introduction to the playtext.
Those early audiences were fortunate, both because they saw
Alec Guinness playing Hilary, and because the twist in the
play would, at least early on in the run, have been a surprise.
Hilary and Bron, both in their early sixties, appear to be living in a country house somewhere in England. There is much
discussion of the landscape and whether it could be Scotland,
Pirbright or Aldershot. They are waiting for a visit from Bron's
sister, Veronica, and her husband, Duff, an oily pillar of the
British establishment. It is not until halfway through the
play, after the arrival of the visitors, that Veronica casually
talks about the heat in Moscow and it becomes clear that this
is more of a country dacha than country cottage. Duff has
come to take Hilary and Bron back to England in exchange
for a British spy.

Hilary is detached and defensive, hiding behind a very
English sense of irony. That's the paradox. Like many other
ex-pats, Hilary, a traitor, dwells on the traditions of the old
country: the Book of Common Prayer; Lyons' tea rooms;
Elgar; and the lending library at the Army and Navy department store. The speech which follows describes the pleasure
he takes in secrets. He recalls a time when he was in the
suburbs delivering classified information to a fellow agent,
when he stumbled across the police searching for a body and

lent a hand in the hunt. He describes how he was acutely aware of the contrast between his own secret, treacherous activities and his outwardly respectable appearance. A man was arrested for the murder of the boy and, unlike Hilary, was not given the chance to flee the country. When Hilary was warned that his cover was about to be blown, his first reaction was to complain about the literary quality of the message.

Hilary It's quite hard to be absolutely alone. I never have.
Though I have seen it. One particular afternoon I had been
on one of my little jaunts, kept my appointment. Nothing
unusual had occurred or was in the least likely to occur.
It was a routine Thursday and I strolled back to the station
across a piece of waste ground that I knew made a nice
short cut. I must have seemed a slightly incongruous figure
in my city clothes. I never dressed the part, even to the
extent of an old raincoat. At which point I came over the
brow of the hill and found myself facing a line of policemen,
advancing slowly through the undergrowth, poking in
ditches with long sticks, hunting for something. It appeared
there was a child missing, believed dead. Clothes had been
found; a shoe. It was a bad moment. I had no reason at all
for being there. I was a senior official in the Foreign Office.
What was I doing on a spring afternoon, with documents
in my briefcase, crossing a common where a child had been
murdered? As it was, no one thought to ask me any
questions at all. I looked too respectable. And indeed they
already had a suspect waiting handcuffed in the police car.
I joined in the search and was with them when they found
the child about half an hour later, lying in a heap at the
foot of a wall. I just got a glimpse of her legs, white, like
mushrooms, before they threw a blanket over her. She had
been dead a week. I saw the man as the police car drew away
through lines of jeering housewives and people cycling
home from work. Then they threw a blanket over him too.
The handy blanket. And I have a feeling he was eventually
hanged. Anyway, it was in those days. I came back, replaced
the documents, had my tea by the fire in the Foreign Office.
I took in some parliamentary questions for the minister,

had dinner at the Garrick and walked home across the park. And in a tiled room at Uxbridge Police Station there would have been that young man waiting. Alone in a cell. Alone in custody. Alone at large. A man without home or haven. That is what you have to do to be cast out. Murder children. Nothing else quite does the trick, because any other crime will always find you friends. Rape them, kill them and be caught.

The Pitchfork Disney

PHILIP RIDLEY

First produced at the Bush, London, in 1991 with Rupert Graves as Presley.

As is clear from this speech, Philip Ridley has a disturbingly gothic imagination, which has more to do with the world of nightmares than everyday life. *The Pitchfork Disney* was the first time he became known as a playwright, although he was already established as a writer of children's stories. The title itself both refers to a nightmare about a serial killer and to a character who arrives towards the end of the play wearing a red sequinned jacket and a bondage mask. Twenty-eight-year-old Presley lives with his twin sister, Hayley, in a state of arrested childhood, feeding on nothing but chocolate and imagining that they are among the few survivors left alive in a post-apocalyptic world. They live behind bolted doors. He is described as 'unshaven, hair unevenly cut very short, skin pale, dark rings beneath bloodshot eyes'. He frequently reminisces about a reassuring, secure past, before their parents disappeared. His current fragile security is shattered when he sees a stranger called Cosmo Disney bending over in pain in the street and invites him into the house. During the conversation that follows, Hayley is flat out, heavily sedated by her brother.

This speech by Presley at the beginning of the play is a typically brazen, schoolboy fantasy taken to extremes. It anticipates Cosmo's revelation that he makes his living by eating live creatures onstage, anything from cockroaches to mice. No wonder Ridley's plays are alarming to watch: the playwright succeeds, like scabies, in getting under one's skin.

Presley I saved my pocket money for three weeks. I didn't buy anything. No comics, no crisps, no sweets. I went to a pet shop and bought this tiny green snake instead. A grass snake they called it. When I got home I played with the snake. It felt warm and soft. I was scared but I still had to hold it. I liked the way it wrapped itself round my fingers like an electric shoelace. And then . . . then I realised. I could never keep it. Not as a pet. Where would it sleep? What would it eat? Where would it go when I went to school? It was a stupid thing to buy. So I had to get rid of it. But how? All sorts of things occurred to me. Flush it down the toilet, bury it, throw it from a tower block. But all the while another thought was taking shape. A thought so wonderful it seemed the only thing to do. So I got a frying pan and put it on the gas stove. I put a bit of butter in the pan and turned the gas up full. The fat started to crackle and smoke. I dropped the snake into the frying pan. It span round and round and its skin burst open like the skin of a sausage. It took ages to die. Its tiny mouth opened and closed and its black eyes exploded. Oh, it was wonderful to watch. All that burning and scalding and peeling. I got a fork and stuck the prongs into its skin. Boiling black blood bubbled out of the holes. When the snake was dead I put it on a plate. I cut the snake into bite-size pieces. I tasted it. Like greasy chicken. I ate it all and licked the plate afterwards. When Mum got home she saw I'd been cooking and hit me. She didn't know anything about the snake. All she was worried about was the scorched patch on the frying pan. She said, 'I'll have to buy a new one now.' But she never did.

The Real Thing

TOM STOPPARD

First produced at the Strand Theatre, London, in 1982 with Roger Rees as Henry.

Henry in *The Real Thing* shares many characteristics with his creator in that he is a successful, witty playwright with a love of pop music and a passionate appreciation of the artist's craft. Tom Stoppard's most intricate and painful play is an examination of the real thing in love, art and politics. Henry's feelings about love and fidelity are changed by his relationship with Annie, an actress, for whom he leaves his wife. His feelings about art, however, don't change. Annie has taken up the cause of Brodie, a man she met on a train when on her way to protest against the siting of American Cruise missiles in England. She is possibly more provoked by the potential closeness of these missiles to her second home than by any political fervour. Brodie is so smitten by her that he follows her to the demonstration, where he is arrested and sent to prison for committing an act of vandalism at the Cenotaph. Annie resolves her guilt by campaigning for his release and encouraging him to write a TV play based on his experiences. His play is full of rage and carries a potent message but is clumsily written, as Henry mockingly points out. Annie admires its raw feeling and believes that Henry's criticisms are snobbish. She wants him to help rewrite it. In this very famous speech, he fetches a cricket bat in order to describe how words should flow with the ease and assurance of a great batsman hitting a ball. Later, for Annie's sake, he does agree to shape Brodie's play but, because he doesn't share the cause, his version is a failure too, but in different ways. One critic wrote about *The Real Thing* at the time of its New York opening that 'it is the best cricket bat anyone has written in years'.

Henry Shut up and listen. This thing here, which looks like a wooden club, is actually several pieces of particular wood cunningly put together in a certain way so that the whole thing is sprung, like a dance floor. It's for hitting cricket balls with. If you get it right, the cricket ball will travel two hundred yards in four seconds, and all you've done is give it a knock like knocking the top off a bottle of stout, and it makes a noise like a trout taking a fly . . .

He clucks his tongue to make the noise.

What we're trying to do is to write cricket bats, so that when we throw up an idea and give it a little knock, it might . . . *travel* . . .

He clucks his tongue again and picks up the script.

Now, what we've got here is a lump of wood of roughly the same shape trying to be a cricket bat, and if you hit a ball with it, the ball will travel about ten feet and you will drop the bat and dance about shouting 'Ouch!' with your hands stuck into your armpits. (*indicating the cricket bat*) This isn't better because someone says it's better, or because there's a conspiracy by the MCC to keep cudgels out of Lords. It's better because it's better. You don't believe me, so I suggest you go out to bat with this and see how you get on. 'You're a strange boy, Billy, how old are you?' 'Twenty, but I've lived more than you'll ever live.' Ooh, ouch!

San Diego

DAVID GREIG

First produced at the Royal Lyceum Theatre, Edinburgh, in August 2003 with Nicholas Pinnock as Andrew.

Playwrights don't usually cast themselves as characters in their own plays. But there are several Davids in *San Diego*, the first of whom is called, like the playwright, David Greig. At the start of the play, he is on a plane making his first trip to America, to San Diego, a city which, he reads, has the highest quality of life of any in the United States. That's not something David gets to experience, since he is stabbed to death, within hours of arriving, by Daniel, a Nigerian immigrant who supposedly travelled on the same plane, only by the more unconventional method of hanging on to one of its wings.

The themes of this weird, ambitious and dreamlike play are concerned with displacement and identity as Greig intricately interweaves a number of narrative strands in a plot that is not without comedy. San Diego is an unsettling place. The Scottish pilot of the flight tries to hire a prostitute called Amy but she can't find her way to his apartment. Two drifters pick up the immigrant and call him Grey Lag after the geese who migrate with rather more sense of purpose than the humans in this play. Back in England, the pilot's daughter, Laura, who is being treated for depression, woos yet another character called David with rissoles created out of her own flesh.

Andrew is Laura's brother, an actor who is filming in the Nevada Desert; by coincidence, his current part is that of a pilot whose plane is hijacked. His wife, Marie, is unsettled by traipsing from film set to film set and is deeply concerned about their baby son whose immune system appears to have broken down. Andrew's father, with whom he has a difficult relationship, visits his son on the set and, in the comic speech that follows, the actor is keen to find out whether the fictional plot of the very duff film he is making bears any relation to his father's reality.

SAN DIEGO

The Nevada Desert.

*Andrew, dressed as a pilot, is talking to the Pilot, who is
also dressed as a pilot.*

They sit at a small table and are drinking bottled beer.

Andrew I'm on a routine flight – to the Gulf – when
suddenly the cockpit door bursts open and this guy comes
in – balaclava over his face – gun – tells me not to panic.
Tells me, 'Stay very, very calm.' I say, 'OK.' He says, 'Right.
Are you calm?' I say, 'I'm calm.' He says, 'Right.' I say,
'Wait a minute. Is anybody hurt out there?' He says, 'Not
yet. Not yet, but we'll shoot the fucking stewardess if you
try any funny business with the fucking plane. Anything the
slightest fucking bit funny we'll shoot her. In fact,' says the
man, 'if you do anything, if this plane does anything that
we don't understand – and we don't understand much
about aeroplanes – so if this plane starts doing something
and we don't know exactly why it's doing that thing, we'll
panic and we'll kill the stewardess. Is that clear?' I say,
'It's clear.' Now, we know each other already from the time
in the airport where I find out who's on my flight and my
eyes go a bit misty when I hear her name. She's called Amy.
Well – what with that moment and the moment when I'm
walking onto the plane and I pass her in the aisle and I say,
'Hello Amy,' and she says, 'Ray . . . it's been a long time,'
and I say, 'Yeah,' and she says – I don't know, some other
shit – so we know that there's a bit of a thing between me
and Amy. So anyway, the hijacker says, 'Take the fucking
plane to fucking Baghdad.' I start plotting the course.
Suddenly, the plane starts emitting this . . . rhythmical sound.
'Thump, thump, thump.' Like great wings beating . . . The

hijackers say, 'What's that?' And I say, 'I don't know,' and then the hijacker says, 'Shoot the stewardess.' The co-pilot tries to overpower them and he gets shot, and I cradle him in my arms, the poor fucker – but the shot's damaged the fucking something or other and we're going down and the there's people being sucked out of the plane and then kaboom – we're crashed in the middle of the fucking sand. After that, it's a kind of Moses thing, as I shepherd the survivors through the desert to Abu Dhabi. Amy survives – and in the desert we fall in love.

Skylight

DAVID HARE

*First produced at the National Theatre, London, in 1995
with Michael Gambon as Tom Sergeant.*

Tom Sergeant is a big bruiser of a man, one of the fashion-
able restaurateurs who revolutionised the English way of
eating and made a fortune for themselves in the eighties. He's
in his fifties, charming, energetic, and very much used to
getting his own way. He turns up one snowy evening in
Kyra's down-at-heel attic flat in Kilburn, London, in the hope
of reigniting an affair that ended some years ago when his
wife discovered that Kyra was more than a friend to her husband. Kyra, who was living in the couple's house at the time,
walked away without telling anyone where she was going.
Fifteen years younger than Tom, Kyra has since made a different life for herself, finding satisfaction in teaching maths
in an under-achieving school in East Ham, making the long
and tedious journey across London in a bus. Tom's wife died
three years ago, and, according to his son, who visits Kyra in
the first scene of the play, his father no longer knows what to
do with himself, but sits at home 'like some stupid animal.
Licking his pain.' Kyra and Tom are full of love for each
other but there is bitterness about the sudden way in which
Kyra left.

   Skylight is an emotionally highly charged, political play,
in which much of the eighties comes under the microscope.
Tom and Kyra no longer share a similar perception of the
world. In this speech, made after the two have been to bed
together, Tom finally explodes, unable to understand the
choices Kyra has made when she could be living in comfort
with him.

Tom You see good in everyone now! How comforting!
Of course. But if I could be reborn as anyone, I'm not sure
Julie Andrews would be my first choice.

*Now it is Tom's turn to go through some sort of barrier,
suddenly losing patience, at last wanting to put an end
to things.*

I mean, Kyra, please! As you'd say: let's be serious! You
must know what's happening. Jesus Christ, just look at this
place! I mean, it is screaming its message. For instance, I tell
you, look at that heater! Sitting there fulfilling some crucial
psychological role in your life. There are shops, I mean, you
know, *shops*, proper shops that exist in the street. These
shops sell heaters. They are not expensive. But of course
they are not what you're looking for. Because these heaters
actually heat!

*Tom shakes his head, moving across the room to get more
Scotch, reaching the real centre of his complaint.*

You accuse *me* of being a monster. You say that I'm guilty.
You tell me that I'm fucking up the life of my horrible son.
But the difference is at least I *admit* it. At least this evening
I took that on board. But you! Jesus! It's like talking to a
moonie. I've not set off like some fucking missionary to
conduct some experiment in finding out just how tough
I can make my own way of life . . .

*But Tom is already behaving as if it were all too
ridiculous for words.*

I mean, I've been listening, I've been listening to this stuff
you've been telling me – the bus! the school! even the kind

of place that you choose to live in – and, I'm thinking, my God, my dear old friend Kyra's joined some obscure religious order. The Kensal Rise chapter! She's performing an act of contrition.

He suddenly laughs, the next thought striking him.

You say to me, Lord goodness, everything's psychological. I can't be happy because I've not come to terms with things that I've done. But you – you're like Page One. A textbook Freudian study! Your whole fucking life is an act of denial! It's so bloody clear. You know what it's called? Throwing Teddy in the corner! You're running so fast you don't even *know* you're in flight.

Take Me Out

RICHARD GREENBERG

*First produced at the Donmar Warehouse, London, in June
2002 with Denis O'Hare as Mason.*

It was a curious decision to premiere Richard Greenberg's
play in London, given that it is about baseball and, on the
whole, the British know as much about baseball as Americans
do about cricket. Mason, a successful, gay accountant, is the
odd one out in a cast of multiracial, professional players, not
all of them very bright. The finest and most famous of them
all is the heroic, good-looking Darren, a self-contained
champion player of mixed race who has only experienced suc-
cess. Unexpectedly, without consulting friends or colleagues,
he announces publicly that he's gay just before the play
starts. His sudden decision confuses everyone, given that he
was not about to be exposed, has no boyfriend and shows
no sign of wanting one. Although the rest of the team dec-
lare that they don't have a problem with his sexuality, they
do start to behave differently towards him, are more self-
conscious and certainly more wary, especially in the changing
room. When the team, usually at the top of the league, unexpectedly starts losing, the manager brings in a new player,
a racial bigot with a disturbed background who complains
on TV about taking a shower with a faggot.

By the end of the play, Darren is disillusioned and the
world of professional baseball has started to look sordid. In
contrast, Mason, Darren's bashful new financial adviser and
a new convert to baseball, romanticises the game and its
players. Mason believes that by coming out Darren has done
a great thing for their shared community. The accountant is
unlike everyone else in the play in that he is more accustomed to slouching in front of a TV than working out in a

gym. Here he explains to Darren why baseball is, he believes, better than democracy.

Mason So I've done what was suggested. I continued to watch and I have come (with no little excitement) to understand that baseball is a perfect metaphor for hope in a democratic society.

It has to do with the rules of play.

It has to do with the mode of enforcement of these rules.

It has to do with certain nuances and grace notes of the game.

First, it's the remarkable symmetry of everything.

All those threes and multiples of threes – calling attention to – virtually making a *fetish* of the game's noble quality.

Equality, that is, of opportunity.

Everyone is given exactly the same chance.

And the opportunity to exercise that chance at his own pace.

There's none of that scurry, none of that relentlessness that marks other games – basketball, football, hockey.

I've never watched basketball, football, or hockey, but I'm sure I wouldn't like them. Or maybe I would, but it wouldn't be the same.

What I mean is, in baseball there's no clock.

What could be more generous than to give everyone all these opportunities and the time to seize them in, as well? And with each turn at the plate, there's the possibility of turning the situation to your favor. Down to the very last try.

And then, to insure that everything remains fair, justices are ranged around the park to witness and assess the play.

And if the justice errs, an appeal can be made.

It's invariably turned down, but that's part of what makes the metaphor so right.

Because even in the most well-meant of systems, error is inevitable. Even within the fairest of paradigms, unfairness will creep in.

And baseball is better than Democracy – or at least than Democracy as it's practiced in this country – because unlike Democracy, baseball acknowledges loss.

While conservatives tell you, leave things alone and no one will lose, and liberals tell you, interfere a lot and no one will lose, baseball says: someone will lose. Not only *says* it – insists upon it!

So that baseball achieves the tragic vision that Democracy evades. Evades *and* embodies.

Democracy is lovely, but baseball's more mature.

Pause.

Another thing I like is the home-run trot.

Not the mad dash around the bases when it's an inside-the-ballpark home run – I'm not sure I've ever *seen* an inside-the-ballpark homerun – I'm talking about that graceful little canter when the ball has been crushed, and it's missing, and the outcome's not in doubt.

What I like about it is it's so unnecessary.

The ball's gone, no one's going to bring it back. And can anyone doubt that a man capable of launching a ball four-hundred feet is somehow going to *fail* to touch a base when he's running uninterfered-with?

For all intents and purposes, the game, at that moment, is not being played.

If duration-of-game is an issue – and I'm given to believe that duration-of-game *is* an issue – the sensible thing would be to say, yes, that's gone, add a point to the score, and send the next batter to the plate.

But that's not what happens.

Instead, play is suspended for a celebration.

A man rounds four bases and, if he's with the home team, the crowd has a catharsis.

And from the way he runs, you learn something about the man. And from the way they cheer, you learn something about the crowd.

And I like this because I don't believe in God.

Or – well – don't *know* about God. Or about any of that . . . metaphysical murk.

Yet, I like to believe that something about being human is . . . good.

And I think what's best about us is manifested in our desire to show respect for one another. For what we can be.

Darren enters, carrying bat.

And that's what we do in our ceremonies, isn't it?

Honor ourselves as we pass through Time?

And it seems to me that to conduct this ceremony not before a game or after a game but in the very *heart* of a game is . . . quite . . . well, does any other game do that?

That's baseball

Tales from Hollywood

CHRISTOPHER HAMPTON

First produced at the Mark Taper Forum Theatre in Los Angeles in 1982; and at the National Theatre, London, in 1983 with Michael Gambon as von Horváth.

Christopher Hampton's play about the European émigrés living in Hollywood during the Second World War was immaculately researched, but still allows itself the luxury of imagining that instead of being killed in a freak accident in Paris in 1938, Odön von Horváth embarked for America. There he joins his other compatriots struggling to make a living writing film scripts for ignorant Hollywood producers. With great wit, Hampton juxtaposes the Europeans' concern about events back home and *Variety*'s parochial interest in the effect of the war on box-office receipts. The main conflict in the play is between the humanism of Horváth, who guides the audience through the action and tries to report life as he sees it, and the more didactic Bertolt Brecht who wants to use his artistic skills to create political change. One of the most striking characters is Nelly, a voluptuous ex-barmaid in her forties, who is married to the seventy-year-old writer Heinrich Mann. Nelly, who married her husband more out of kindness than love, can't cope with exile, cuckolds her husband and takes to the bottle. She makes a pass at Horváth, who is younger than most of the German writers, but his fondness and respect for Mann makes him turn her down. Knowing her affection for Horváth, Mann asks him to help when Nelly gets into trouble with the police but there is little that he can do. The last time he and Nelly meet, she tells him about the affair she is having with a boy who not only doesn't love her but also treats her with indifference and brutality. Horváth can do nothing to help her.

Horváth Before I left, Heinrich told me he'd disposed of all her sleeping pills. But she fooled him.

> *As he speaks, Nelly makes her way over to Heinrich's desk. She pours herself a glass of water from the carafe, then opens a drawer and brings out a bottle of pills. She starts taking handfuls of them, moving quickly. When she finishes, she drops the bottle into the waste-paper basket and lies down, curling up on the stage in a foetal position.*

And so the whole weary scene was played again. But this time with a difference.

> *As he continues, Heinrich comes back into the room. He rushes over to Nelly and drops to one knee beside her. Then, as Horváth's story moves towards its climax, strobe lighting. In its harsh glare, Heinrich can be seen grappling with Nelly's body, heaving it up and struggling across the room with it, as if in some appalling dance.*

He bundled her into a taxi and got her to the nearest hospital. But they were very busy, as it was just before Christmas, and they didn't like the look of this shabby old foreigner, who didn't have enough money on him, and they refused to take his cheque. So he had to call another taxi and set off to another hospital, where they were regretfully forced to take the same attitude, but at least told him of a third hospital, where he might expect better luck. He'd kept the taxi waiting this time, just in case, so they were able to speed off without delay to hospital number three, where indeed they were far more helpful and were able to tell him right away that Nelly had just died.

The strobe cuts out. Heinrich and Nelly vanish, and the spot isolates Horváth.

A few weeks before, I had been to a fund-raising meeting for Roosevelt in Bel Air. Thomas Mann, who was now an American citizen, spoke. He appeared sandwiched between a conjuror who told an interminable story about a Chinese called Rosenthal and a lady ventriloquist; and was marginally less well received than either. All the same, you could tell that America had taken him to its heart. And from then on, whenever I thought about America, the two images, one seen and one imagined, rose before me: Thomas, on that white podium in that manicured garden; and Heinrich, weeping and covered with vomit, pleading with the admissions clerk in some casualty department, trying to get some attention paid to his dying wife.

Silence.

The York Realist

PETER GILL

*First produced by the English Touring Theatre at the Lowry,
Salford Quays , in 2001 with Lloyd Owen as George.*

Peter Gill's play looks back forty years to his own youth,
when he was a director at the Royal Court, discovering and
presenting the plays of D. H. Lawrence, scrupulous portraits of
working-class life in Eastwood, near Nottingham. Lawrence's
detailed realism is present in Gill's play, too. The play is set
in the early sixties when John, a young director, travels up to
York to assist in an amateur staging of the York Mystery
Plays. Nobody knows who wrote this cycle, but the author
has become known as the York Realist for the way in which
he took the Biblical characters of the Middle East and turned
them into down-to-earth characters from the north of England.
In the cast is George, a gifted amateur actor by night, and a
farm labourer by day. John and George are attracted to each
other, and when George fails to turn up for a rehearsal, the
director arrives unexpectedly at the remote tied cottage George
shares with his mother. The two begin an affair that is spar-
ingly represented by a kiss onstage. Even so, because of cen-
sorship, the play would have been impossible to stage at the
time in which it is set. Interestingly, Gill shows that George
is relaxed about his homosexuality and that the rest of his
family, rather than being outraged, chooses to turn a blind
eye. At the time the play is set, northern actors, such as Tom
Courtenay and Albert Finney, were all the rage, and John is
eager for George to join him in London where he believes his
lover will be able to find work as an actor. Much as George
enjoys his trip to the capital, class and education make him
feel an outsider. Even after his mother's death he can't make the
break, and the affair ends. In this speech, he tries to explain

to John how he feels about London and about how the arts, sadly, aren't really for people like him.

George I did [like London]. I did. It was all right. It was great for a visit. All the visits. But what would I do? Where would I live? In your little room, sleeping in that three-quarter bed? I liked it. You know I did. They were all friendly, your friends. All of them.

And all the things to do. That we did. The picture galleries. That picture house on Oxford Street. The National Film Theatre. All the theatres and the concerts and the chat and everything. The white rooms and brass beds my mother said they had when she was a child. And the white Japanese lampshades and bookcases made out of bricks and planks. And the Whitechapel Gallery and American paintings and the deal tables and the bentwood chairs and the crocheted shawls.

And they were friendly. Very friendly people. Mad-heads, half of them. And the real coffee. Ugh. And the red wine, worse. And dinner in the night. I liked most of all that play on a Sunday. That was right good. Nearly a fight there was over that. What a lot they were. And the ballet. The ballet. Me. That curtain swinging up. All of it. And they were all nice too. And I enjoyed it all because you did. I'd do owt for you. But what would I do? Where would I work?

Acknowledgements

All plays are published by Faber and Faber Ltd and/or
Faber Inc. unless otherwise stated. The editor and publishers
gratefully acknowledge the permission to reproduce
copyright material in this book.

The extracts included in this book may be performed in
class and for auditions, festivals and examination without
further permission or payment. However, should you wish
to perform any scene in a public performance such as a
festival, prizewinners' concert or an entertainment involving
the selling of tickets, further permission must be obtained
from the correct source. In addition, if you wish to perform
a play in part or in its entirety you must seek permission
first. No performance can be given unless a licence has first
been obtained. You will find full details inside the published
text and it is essential to adhere to the rules.

As a general rule, the publisher Samuel French Limited
controls the amateur performing rights for plays it publishes
as well as the amateur rights for many plays professionally
controlled by others. Their address is: Samuel French
Limited, 52 Fitzroy Street, London WIP 6JR.

'Art' © Yasmina Reza, 1994, translation © Yasmina Reza
and Christopher Hampton, 1996; Bash © Neil LaBute,
1999 (originally published in the USA by the Overlook
Press); Butley © Simon Gray, 1971; Comedians © Trevor
Griffiths, 1976, 1979; A Day in the Death of Joe Egg
© Peter Nichols, 1967; Dogs Barking © Richard Zajdlic,
1999; East © Steven Berkoff, 1977, 1978, 1982, 1989,
2000; Faith Healer © Brian Friel, 1980; Frozen © Bryony
Lavery, 2002; Gagarin Way © Gregory Burke, 2001;
The Hothouse © Harold Pinter, 1980; Howard Katz